Contents

CW01662937

Department of the Environment
Ancient Monuments and Historic Buildings

2

Lindisfarne Priory

NORTHUMBERLAND

by the late
A. HAMILTON THOMPSON
C B E, D Litt, LL D, F B A, F S A, Hon A R I B A

LONDON: HER MAJESTY'S STATIONERY OFFICE

First published 1949
Tenth impression 1975

ISBN 0 11 670132 3

History

The isle of Lindisfarne was given by Oswald after his conquest of Bernicia in 634 to Aidan, the missionary bishop sent from Iona, to be the see of his diocese. Here, within sight of the royal vill of Bamburgh and separated from the mainland by a strait passable at low tide, a monastery was founded on the Irish pattern, ruled over by an abbot, but in which the bishop resided when not engaged in travelling with the King on their joint work of evangelisation.

Although under the rule of Oswiu, the brother and successor of Oswald, York recovered the position of capital—civil and ecclesiastical—of Northumbria which it had held before the death of Edwin and the flight of Paulinus in 633, the see and monastery of Lindisfarne continued to exist for over 240 years. After the acceptance of the Roman Easter at the synod of Whitby in 664, the champions of the Celtic Easter left the monastery for Scotland, and the most famous of the bishops of Lindisfarne, Cuthbert, himself a Scot, ruled (685–87) in a church which conformed to the general practice of western Christendom and over a diocese which had been reduced in area by the foundation of a new bishopric at Hexham.

With the exception of a few carved stones of a date later than the period of Cuthbert, no traces of the early church and monastery survive at Lindisfarne. Their place in the history of English culture is represented by two manuscripts, now in the British Museum, the Lindisfarne Gospels, a masterpiece of seventh-century art, and the lists of names, written in characters alternately of gold and silver, in the *Liber Vitae* which afterwards lay for centuries on the high-altar of Durham Cathedral, and by the wooden coffin of St Cuthbert and its contents, now in the Library of the Dean and Chapter at Durham. The exposed position of Lindisfarne laid it open to attacks from pirates. It was the scene of the first descent of the Danes upon the English coast, when on 7 June 793 they sacked the monastery and murdered most of its inmates. In spite of this the succession of bishops and abbots was preserved and the monastic tradition carried on until 875, when the congregation of St Cuthbert, led by their bishop Eardwulf and their abbot Eadred, and bearing with them the stone sarcophagus which contained the body of St Cuthbert and the head of St Oswald, fled before the second Danish onslaught. After seven years of wandering, productive of much legendary incident, they settled at Chester-le-Street in 882. There the see remained fixed for 113 years, until in 995, again from fear of the Danes, Aldhun, twenty-fourth bishop in succession from St Aidan, migrated with all his people and with the cherished relics. This time their wanderings brought them to Durham, which thus became the permanent see of the successors of Aidan and Cuthbert.

In 1069–70, when the Conqueror was preparing to take vengeance upon Durham for the murder there by the Northumbrians of their earl Robert Cumin, the bishop and the throng of both sexes which constituted the congregation of St Cuthbert took flight to Lindisfarne, and the saint's body returned for a while to the home which it had quitted nearly two centuries before. Their stay, however, was short and they were back in Durham by 25 March 1070, when their church, polluted and desecrated, was reconciled for divine worship.

With the advent of the Norman bishop, William of Saint-Calais (*de S Carilefo*), to Durham in 1081 and the conversion of the cathedral establishment into a Benedictine monastery, the sacred site of Lindisfarne became the property of the prior and convent of Durham. The ruins which we see today are those of the cell or priory which they founded there. Like other cells of Durham, it was tenanted by monks sent there from the mother-house and governed by priors who were deputies appointed by the priors of Durham, and it remained in this subordinate position throughout its history. With the foundation of the new priory the name of Holy Island appears to have come into general use and practically superseded that of Lindisfarne.

What the monks from Durham found at Lindisfarne we do not know. There was probably a church, possibly the remains of the early monastic church, on the spot, and a monk named Edward is said to have built a new church from the foundations about this period. This, however, may well have been the parish church, distinct from the monastic church and rebuilt in its present form during the thirteenth century. It was the mother church of the district known as Islandshire, which before 1145 included the mainland chapelries of Ancroft, Lowick, Kyloe and Tweedmouth, and it appears likely that it acquired this status during the interval between the Danish invasions and the revival of monastic life at Lindisfarne. In any case, the priory church itself was begun not very long after the settlement from Durham, and the date of its beginning is approximately contemporary with that of the first great building campaign at Durham (1093–1104).

The internal history of the priory is uneventful. The names of its priors are known chiefly from the monastic account-rolls of Durham

The church from the south-west

and from the rolls and inventories, preserved at Durham, which belonged to the cell. Some of these names are well known: Henry Luceby, prior in 1300, was the prior forced by Bishop Bek shortly afterwards upon the convent of Durham, and William Ebchester, prior of Durham 1446–56, had been prior of Holy Island 1430–37. The series of account-rolls, beginning in 1360, affords a continuous source of information on the financial and economic condition of the priory until the Dissolution, while the inventories supply suggestions for the use of rooms, of which remains exist, in the monastic buildings, belonging to the late medieval period and corresponding to no regular features of the monastic plan.

Holy Island was a place of call on the sea-route from Newcastle to Berwick and was often used as a convenient port by the royal officers responsible for the collection of victuals and other materials for the King's use. During the Scottish wars of the fourteenth century it was continually in danger of raids. It was, however, well protected: the

Heugh, a basaltic ridge south of the priory, formed a natural shield for the monastery and haven, and a small fort was built upon it. The priory precinct was also partly fortified and so was the outcrop of basalt known as the Beblowe at the south-east end of the island which commanded a wide outlook over the open sea. The small fortress which occupies its summit was not built until the reign of Henry VIII, when it possibly took the place of some earlier lookout-tower. If the island was fairly secure, Scottish marauders did much damage in the coastal district dependent upon the priory. An appeal for temporary relief from the prior and convent of Durham to the Crown in 1381, owing to the devastation of Islandshire and the lands of Coldingham priory, another of their dependencies, was no isolated instance of the harm wrought by border forays.

Shortly before the dissolution of the priory in 1537, the last prior, Thomas Sparke, consecrated bishop suffragan of Berwick in the same year, had received a lease for life from the prior and convent of Durham of the site and buildings with other property in the island. He continued in occupation and after the transference of Holy Island to the newly founded dean and chapter of Durham, his lease was confirmed by the Crown in 1543. He sub-let it, however, to the King's surveyor of victuals at Berwick; the church was turned into a storehouse and in 1550 the buildings were in bad condition, the south-east wall of the brewhouse was reported as "very weak" and general decay seems to have been imminent. Sparke, who probably resided on his prebend at Durham, did not die until 1571, when the reversion of his lease passed to Sir William Reed of Fenham by virtue of a grant made in 1564. The rights of ownership in the property were further complicated by a grant of the royalties of the see of Durham in Norhamshire and Islandshire made by James I, with the reluctant consent of Bishop Matthew, to George Hume, Earl of Dunbar. From the earl these royalties descended to his second daughter and co-heiress, Elizabeth, wife of Theophilus Howard, Lord Walden and eventually second Earl of Suffolk. In 1613, Lord Walden took advantage of this and of rival claims to proprietorship to remove the leaden roofs of the priory buildings. The lead, on its way southward, was sunken by a storm at sea, but Lord Walden came victorious out of the suit which followed his assertion of his regalian rights, and the dean and chapter of Durham were ousted from the property which they claimed in virtue of their foundation charter.

The severance of the long connection of Lindisfarne with Durham left the priory a complete ruin, and subsequently the island was held by successive lessees of the royalties from the Crown. Its occupation by a royalist force in 1643, and by supporters of the Pretender in 1715, are incidents which lie outside the history of the priory and belong to that of the castle on the Beblowe. The excavation of the priory buildings was begun in 1888 by Sir William Crossman and, since their transference to the Office of Works (now the Department of the Environment), the whole site has been cleared.

Description

The site of the priory, enclosed by a wall, is divided into two parts. The church, with the cloister on its south side, occupied the higher ground to the north: the outer court occupied the southward slope and hollow between the cloister buildings and the steeply rising hill called the Heugh. A gateway in the wall marks the site of the original gatehouse in the north-west corner of the outer court. The west doorway of the church, entered from the graveyard of the parish church, through which the buildings are now approached, was intended merely for ceremonial use, and the doorway through which lay folk had access to the nave was in the north wall, beyond the original limits of the parochial churchyard.

CHURCH

The buildings belong entirely to the period after the Norman Conquest, and the church, probably begun in the last years of the eleventh, was completed within the first half of the twelfth century. It was planned with a short chancel and apse, the foundations of which remain within the walls of the present chancel. The idea that this is a remnant of a pre-Conquest church is without proof and the plan corresponds closely to that of the east end of Whitby Abbey as revealed by excavation, the date of which is nearly contemporary with that of the settlement from Durham at Lindisfarne. Subsequently, in the second half of the twelfth century, the place of this early chancel was taken by a square-ended presbytery of three bays. West of this the piers of the transept-crossing carried a tower, with short transepts north and south, each with an apsidal chapel on the east side. The nave was of six bays with north and south aisles. The whole building is of massive Romanesque construction and after the twelfth century received no structural addition, alterations being confined to the insertion of a few Gothic windows. Externally, the bays are divided by pilaster buttresses which, save at the east end, do not project beyond the plinth of the walls. At the angles of the east wall the buttresses, set in pairs at right angles, project boldly and the plinth is carried round them. The buttresses between the east and second bays of the chancel also project noticeably and in comparatively modern times two buttresses on each side of the chancel were strengthened by the addition of heavy blocks of masonry. The apsidal chapels of the transept have rounded pilasters, four in each wall, which were probably carried up to the eaves. In the west angles of the nave, large square turrets, projecting outward and inward and enclosing spiral stairs to the upper parts of the church, were entered from the interior of the building.

Some of the architectural detail, notably the internal arcading in the wall above the west doorway, is rude and primitive, but in the nave the imitation of work at Durham is obvious, while the ribbed vaulting with which the church was covered clearly followed the example set by Durham. The advanced detail of the vaulting-rib which spans the crossing suggests a date not earlier than 1140, while the chancel was not fully finished on its present scale till considerably later.

The chancel or presbytery, without aisles, was lighted in the two western bays by round-headed windows with slight inward splays, two on either side in each bay, with a clerestory and wall-passage above. The two windows in the south wall of the west bay remain, one blocked: on the north side one remains, but the other is broken away. The east bay had no lateral windows and the place of those in the east wall was taken in the fourteenth century by a large traceried window, probably of five lights, the arch of which is perfect but the tracery gone. At the same period windows, apparently of three lights and now in like condition, were inserted in both walls of the middle bay. Of the clerestory only traces are left: the walls were heightened in the fifteenth century, when the roof was probably flattened and a chamber possibly made, as at Tynemouth and Brinkburn, between it and the vaulting. The corbelled springers of the chancel vault remain: the diagonals sprang from shafts with capitals set in the direction of the ribs, a feature which does not occur in the Durham vaults, where the capitals are set parallel to the wall. In the eastern bay, which is narrower than the others, the corbels and springers are at a higher level than those to the west. A trefoil-headed piscina was inserted in the south wall of the eastern bay in the thirteenth century, and a locker in the north wall. A passage, apparently original, from the chancel to the apsidal chapel in the north transept, cuts through an angle of the north-east crossing-pier.

The four piers of the crossing were cruciform in shape, with a shaft between two lesser shafts on each face. The main shafts have cushion capitals. Only the base and lower courses of the north-east pier and the plinth of the south-west pier remain. The other pair stand for their full height, and above them are the springings of the west and south arches of the crossing, which was vaulted upon diagonal ribs with chevron mouldings, springing from the level of the adjoining clerestory passages. One of the ribs, with the keystone, remains entire owing to the preservation of the abutting walls of the chancel and north transept, above the angles of which rise the lower courses of the former tower.

The transepts were approximately square, projecting for half their area beyond the aisles of the nave. The west wall of the north transept remains for most of its height, with the arches opening into the adjoining aisle and triforium of the nave. The upper part of the wall was lighted by a single window of which the lower part remains. In the north west angle a square turret was built for the stair which led to the clerestory wall passage and the tower. Next to this the north wall rises as far as the gable, but its eastern part has gone above the sill of a large round-headed window of which the west jamb and part of the arch remain. The east wall and that of the apsidal chapel to the east have disappeared from a similar level.

The south transept retains the lower parts of the west and south walls, in the angle between which is the internal projection from which the night-stair ascended to the dorter and was probably continued upwards. In the middle of the south wall is a doorway into the adjoining eastern range of the cloister. The east wall, though much ruined, remains for most of its height, and the wide arch of the apse, with coupled jamb-shafts, stands entire. The apse itself, with a portion of its vault, is partly standing; but there is a wide gap where the wall was pierced by a single light. The mark of its outer roof is on the outer face of the transept wall, the upper part of which was lighted by a single window.

The nave was of six bays. All but the plinth and lowest courses of the south wall have gone, and of the south arcade only the west respond, part of the base of the next pier to the east and the plinths of two other piers remain. Of the north arcade the two east bays and west respond are complete. As at Durham, major piers of cruciform shape with attached shafts alternated with circular piers. In the third bay there is a well, the head of which projects beyond the line of the piers into the nave. The major pier between the fourth and fifth bays is ruined to the plinth, but the lower parts of the two circular piers on either side remain. The circular piers are ornamented with incised designs of the same type as those at Durham. The triforium and clerestory have entirely disappeared save for slight remains against the north-west crossing-pier and on both sides of the west front. The triforium is known to have had a wide arch subdivided into two openings, and the clerestory had a wall-passage, probably with a single window-opening in each bay. The vaulting-ribs sprang from shafts or corbels near the

The nave of the church, looking west

springing of the triforium arches. Against the west front the line of the vault just clears the level of the upper window. Probably, as at Durham, transverse arches crossed the nave above the major piers, but were omitted above the intermediate piers.

The whole of the five eastern bays of the north wall with responds corresponding in design to the piers of the arcade is standing, but the upper part of the west bay has gone. The springers of the vaulting-ribs of the aisle remain: the transverse arch between the second and third bays and the arch into the transept are entire. Each bay was lighted by a single window splayed inwards, which in the fourth bay was raised above a doorway, now blocked. The blocking of this and the cloister doorway opposite probably indicate the disuse of the nave during the century before the suppression of the priory. For this doorway the arch remains in the outer wall, which was thickened flush with the adjacent buttresses. In the fourteenth century a three-light window was inserted in the east bay. In both aisles the west bay was constricted by the intrusion of the turrets at the west angles of the nave.

The original masonry of the south wall seems to have been disturbed at various points, and inserted masonry in the fourth bay indicates that there was a doorway here opposite that in the north wall. The only complete buttress on this side is at the back of the westernmost vaulting-shaft, but the footings of the others remain.

The west front of the church is pierced by a round-headed doorway, the outer arch of which, contained in a bold projection from the wall, is of three orders with chevron mouldings and shafts with cubical capitals in the jambs. On either side of it there are two arched recesses with shafts in the wall-face, and at each end of the wall the square turrets project, but not so far as the projection for the doorway, to which the whole design is subordinated. Beyond this portal the passage through the thickness of the wall is widened slightly for the inner arch, of two orders, which has lost its shafts. Above the doorway there is externally a wide round-headed window with jamb-shafts, at the level of the capitals of which a string-course, continued along the turrets, divided this part of the wall-face into two stages. At the back of the window there is a passage in the walls, opening to the church by an inner arcade of five tall unmoulded arches divided by thick shafts with cubical capitals and square bases. In the third storey there is a tall round-headed window with external and internal shafts. Here there was no wall passage: the outer wall face was recessed between broad pilasters, while internally the head of the window thrust itself into the curve of the vault.

Above the vault the original gable of the west front was removed in the fourteenth century and the wall on each side was heightened and the roof raised. This formed part of the defensive additions to the monastery, to which also belong the two crossbow-loops beneath the ruined gable. The turrets at each end of the west front were divided by string-courses into six stages, the internal stairs being lighted at intervals by small loops. In the east face of the south turret, which is perfect for four stages and part of the fifth, the mark of the sloping roof of the nave triforium is visible. Its staircase above the lowest steps is broken away. Of the north turret only the lower part of the ground stage remains.

As regards ritual arrangements, the choir occupied the transept-crossing, and slots in the north-west pier mark the position of the *pulpitum* at its west end. The site of the rood-screen is similarly marked in the first circular pier on the north side of the nave.

CLOISTER

No part of the cloister buildings is contemporary with the church. The permanent community of monks was never large and the first buildings for their accommodation were probably small. Indications of the pillared undercroft of a frater on the south side of the cloister suggest that the original cloister was square and that in the thirteenth century it was enlarged upon an oblong plan with the longer axis from north to south. Foundations of the outer walls of the cloister walks remain on three sides, but there seems to have been no north walk next the church, for the west wall, which is not parallel to that of the adjoining range of building, slanted in a north-easterly direction as it approached the church, and there is now only a narrow space between its end and the church wall. Of the east wall the only foundations are those of the south part, and on this side the walk was no more than a narrow passage closed at its south end by a door. In the fourteenth century the south walk was partly incorporated in the frater and its west end was blocked by a large mass of masonry, while a doorway from the screens between the frater and the block of domestic offices at its west end gave access to the west walk.

The whole arrangement of the cloister shows a transition from the regular monastic plan to a plan of a frankly domestic type. The cloister

Tombstone in the museum

walks were simply covered passages in front of the buildings, and can have been of little use for study or contemplation, while after their complete interruption in the fourteenth century they were rendered useless for processions. Further, the fortification of the buildings was responsible for additional features which make them still more unlike those of an ordinary monastery.

EAST RANGE

The east range of the cloister adjoined the south transept, but on a slightly different axis. It was of two storeys, with the dorter on the upper floor over a sub-vault of four bays, vaulted from half-rounded shafts in the angles and against the walls. The east wall, slightly set back from that of the transept, remains for part of its height, standing upon a thicker foundation: at its south end there is the lower part of a single-light window which was blocked outside by a garderobe added when the dorter was rebuilt in the fifteenth century. The foundations of the west wall correspond to the thick foundation of the other wall, projecting beyond and continued round the angle of the transept. All traces of doorways from the cloister have disappeared. The doorway from the transept opened into the north end of the sub-vault, the

first bay of which, partitioned off from the rest, formed a vestry. The second and third bays must have been the chapter-house. There is no sign of a partition between them and the fourth bay, in the south wall of which there is a doorway into the adjoining range. Neither here nor in the church is there any trace of a way to the monks' graveyard, in which several interments remain.

The dorter has been destroyed, but, as already said, the foot of the night stair into the church remains; the day stair was approached through the doorway at the south end of the east cloister walk, where the passage was contracted by the thickening of the angle of the dorter range. Beyond this a lobby on the left hand led to the foot of the stair, which ascended in the south wall of the range.

SOUTH RANGE

The whole of the south range of the cloister with the large blocks of buildings which project east and west was greatly altered and for the most part rebuilt and enlarged in the fourteenth century. These changes converted it into a large house of which the hall was the frater, while —as in an ordinary dwelling-house—there was at one end of the hall a block of living-rooms and at the other end a block containing the domestic offices. Both of these blocks encroached upon and included buildings which actually belonged to the east and west cloister ranges.

PARLOUR AND DAY STAIR

Beyond the parlour, into which there is a doorway in the south wall of the sub-vault, the east range originally continued southward to a wall of thirteenth-century date continuous with the outer wall of the frater. The parlour was a vaulted chamber altered in the fourteenth century. In the north-west corner is the lobby of the day stair already described, south of which there are remains of a doorway which opened into the enlarged frater. A doorway in the south wall opens into the ground-floor room of the prior's lodging. Of two doorways in the east wall the southern is the earlier; when the chimney of the prior's lodging was built, it was blocked up, and the new doorway in the north-east corner of the parlour was made.

PRIOR'S LODGING

The construction of the prior's new lodging, which appears in the accounts of 1341–42, was accompanied by the construction or remodelling of rooms further east and by the building of a fortified wall which enclosed the eastern part of these buildings and the space east of the parlour, and from a half-octagon tower at its north end was continued westward to the south end of the dorter range. The site east of the parlour seems to have been left open.

Before the fourteenth-century alterations the wall at the south end of the dorter range was adjoined by a chamber for the prior to the east, the stair to which was utilised in the new lodging. East of this was the infirmary building, approached by the south-east doorway of the parlour through an open passage with the wall of the prior's *camera* to the south and a wall on the north of which the foundations partly remain. This may have been the south wall of the reredorter, east of and at right angles to the dorter range. The reredorter, however, must have been curtailed or done away with when the fortified wall was built, and, as the parlour doorway was now blocked, the new doorway opened into a narrow passage in the north part of its ground floor by which access might be had to the infirmary.

The new prior's lodging, absorbing the south end of the dorter range, was divided into two floors. On the ground floor was a large room, which was probably used as a warming-house, with its longer axis from east to west, entered from the parlour at its north-west corner. At the south end of its west wall there was a doorway into the frater. In the north wall there is a large open fireplace, the chimney of which is perfect, and close to this in the east wall there is a doorway to the buildings beyond. The upper floor was reached by the spiral stair in the south wall preserved from the older lodging, east of the opening of which there is a blocked doorway. The upper chamber has a fireplace in its north wall, to the west of the fireplace below, with a flue sloping upwards into the main shaft.

Of the two chambers that on the ground floor may well have been the common-room or warming-house (*calefactorium*), which in a Benedictine house was usually at the south end of the east range, while the chamber above was the prior's private room, possibly partitioned into study and bedroom. The prior's chapel, mentioned in the inventories, was obviously on the same floor, probably a small oratory either in a room above the parlour or to the east of the chamber. The arrangement of common-room with *camera* above is precisely that familiar in the collegiate plans of the later middle ages, in which the master's lodging was on the floor above the common-room of the fellows.

INFIRMARY

The north wall of the infirmary, continuous with that of the common-room, has mostly gone. There are no traces of an infirmary hall or of a stair to an upper floor, and, as the infirmary disappears from the inventories after 1341–42, it is possible that after the alterations of that period an infirmary was dispensed with. Nor do the inventories afford any clue to the use of the two rooms east of the common-room, the larger of which at the east end has a hearth in the floor. Their south wall stands clear of the fortified wall, which was built outside it and runs eastward to an angle-turret or bartisan corbelled out externally, but with a square inward projection in which is a garderobe shaft. The outer wall continues along the east side of the chamber with the hearth to the half-octagon tower, a massive building now ruined almost to the ground, which projected deeply into the space behind. There is a rectangular outward projection from the east wall at the end near the tower. From the tower, as already described, the wall, here very thick, goes westward to the dorter range, the outer angle at their junction being filled by the later garderobe which has been mentioned.

The west doorway of the church

FRATER

The refectory or frater, with its longer axis from east to west, occupied the south side of the cloister. Its south wall, in the east part of which there is a wide gap, is of the thirteenth century. In the following century the east wall, common to the frater and the prior's lodging, was rebuilt. In its south wall a window-sill is embedded. Part, at any rate, of the north wall was removed and the adjoining cloister walk was blocked. Foundations on this side are fragmentary and uncertain, but there are indications that an extension of the frater at its north-east corner was made to the doorway at the end of the east cloister walk, thus taking in the angle of the cloister. This extension may very well have been the "lavatory suspended" (*sic*) mentioned in 1533 and may have been screened off from the frater. The west end of the former cloister walk was filled with a large block of masonry, the inner face of which is that of the thirteenth-century frater wall. Its south-east angle is broken away. The conjecture that this was the base of the frater pulpit is improbable alike from its size and its situation, and it seems likely that in the broken part there were steps leading to a stair and landing giving access to the upper part of the west buildings.

KITCHEN, BREWHOUSE AND BAKEHOUSE

At the south end of the screens (the transverse passage at the west end of the frater) was the doorway by which the cloister buildings were entered from the outer court, while at its north end was the doorway to the west walk of the cloister. In the west wall of the screens there were three doorways, all of thirteenth-century date. Of these the middle one opened into a passage, those on each side into rooms. The south room, which had a second doorway from the passage, is square with fireplaces in the west and south walls. The north room had a barrel vault running north and south with transverse ribs, contracted at the north-east corner by the internal projection of a staircase from the cloister to the upper floor. Near its north-west corner there is a pit in the floor. A splayed opening in the west wall is partly blocked by the later building beyond, and a wider window-opening was made close by on the south. Originally this room had no doorway to the west, but, when the large block of buildings on this side was added in the fourteenth century, the middle passage was disused, and a party wall with a doorway in it converted the south end of the chamber into a through-passage opening into the new building. The middle passage was now blocked towards the screens of the frater, but was otherwise left open, and it is probable that the doorway from it to the south chamber was made at this time.

The fourteenth-century building has very thick walls, but without towers or turrets at the angles. Its south-west corner adjoined the gate-house of the monastery, and at the other end of the south wall, where it joined the earlier buildings just described, there was a doorway from the outer court. This led into a paved area in the south-west angle of which is a platform, carrying a brick-lined structure for a large boiler which was approached by steps in the projecting masonry on the north side. Between this projection and the inner wall of another paved area in the north-east part of the building there was a doorway and a short passage to a large chamber which had a hearth in the middle and a sink in the floor against the east wall. The drain from this, with a portion of the lead pipe, lies open where it crosses the north end of the frater screens. At the north end of this chamber there are remains of steps down to a circular sinking in the floor for a mash-tub or brewing-lead. East of it was an open paved area, entered at its south-east corner by the passage made in the south end of the barrel-vaulted chamber. At the north-east corner there is in the north wall a brick-lined recess for an oven, which interfered with a window from the same chamber and, as already noted, caused the making of a new window. There is no trace of a fireplace next the oven.

The buildings just described were evidently the brewhouse and bake-house constantly mentioned in the monastic accounts. The whole group including the earlier buildings to which they were added, with the west cloister range, seems to be covered by the inclusion of the cellar, larder, kitchen, brewhouse and bakehouse in an inventory made in 1347. The normal position of the cellar was in the west range. The barrel-vaulted chamber next the cellar was the larder, and the pit in the floor may be the cistern for the larder which was "made anew" in 1451–52. The chamber with the fireplaces south of the earlier passage from the frater was thus the kitchen.

WEST RANGE

The west alley of the cloister was entered from the north end of the frater screens. Its outer wall, as previously noted, was not parallel to the wall of the west range and diverges considerably from it at its north end.

West end of the church interior

The ground floor of the west range, which belongs to the thirteenth-century work, was originally one long cellar extending from the north wall of the larder to the south-west turret of the church and probably was divided into three compartments by wooden partitions. The west wall was pierced by six splayed loops which still remain. At a later date the partitions were superseded by walls, one of which blocked, while the other impinged upon, a window in the outer wall. In the cloister walk, near the end of the east wall of the larder, is the foot of a staircase leading to the upper floor, of the arrangements of which nothing remains except two deep garderobe pits, set side by side in a square block at the south end of the west wall. The upper floor may have been used for servants' rooms in the later days of the monastery. Beyond the staircase the wall of the west range is recessed for some distance and contains a doorway to a room with a barrel vault east and west which was inserted when the partition wall was built. Beyond the cross-wall the wall is thickened, but is again recessed to a doorway leading into the second room, which, with the third, was covered by a barrel vault running north and south with transverse ribs. The wall continues to the church without further thickening and contains a doorway to the third room. Between the second and third doorways there is a piece of foundation in front of the wall which may mark the position of a projecting trough or lavatory, for not far south of this point a wide paved drain, pursuing a curving course, to which a pipe may have been laid from the trough, escapes through the outer wall of the cloister walk in a south-easterly direction. Of the three rooms in the west range one may have been the buttery. The buttery is out of its usual place in the house-plan, but it is probable that the pantry, mentioned in 1401 and 1416, and the buttery, first mentioned in 1481, were identical, and this seems a reasonable position for such a room.

OUTER COURTYARD

In the fourteenth century a barbican, formed by two parallel walls running southward, was built in front of the south entrance to the frater screens. The south part of the space thus enclosed was a paved open porch, from which the inner porch was entered by a door opening inwards, the bar-hole of which remains. The rest of the space is cobbled.

On the east side of the outer court the enclosing wall runs southward for 60ft from the projection formed by the spiral stair to the first floor of the building east of the frater. It has been thickened on the inner side, and there are traces of original openings in the outer face which were blocked by the inner layer of masonry. The wall then proceeds for 25ft to an angle buttress formed by two projections at right angles to each other. This part of it is the east wall of a building projecting into the court with its major axis from east to west and a doorway in the north-east corner, the ground floor of which was divided by party walls into three chambers. The east chamber was paved with slabs; the second, at a lower level, was cobbled. Of the west chamber only part of the foundations remains.

From the buttress at the south-east angle of this building the outer wall turns westward for 10ft and then runs for 60ft to the south-west corner of the enclosure, forming the outer wall of a building, with its major axis north and south, at right angles to the last building described. It is then returned for 25ft with a slight south-westerly inclination to the point of junction with the buildings on the south side of the court. The east wall, pierced by four narrow loops splayed internally, is for 43ft a facing added to an older wall and cut through to the splays of three of these loops. Between the third and fourth loops there is a cross wall, beyond which the older part of the wall ends, and the south end, with its westward return, enclosed a room measuring internally 16ft east to west by 11½ft north to south and lighted by the fourth loop near its north-east corner. This room ended on the west side in a wall which joins the cross wall near its west end and is thickened where it meets the outer wall, in which there may have been at this point a doorway opening into a narrow space between the room and the south range of buildings.

The lining of the east wall and its extension beyond the cross wall indicates the enlargement of an earlier building in the fourteenth century. In the middle of the west wall of the long room there is a projection for an outer stair which mounted against the wall southward. This building was probably a guest-house with hall and chamber on the upper floor, while the loops lighted the cellars below. The part south of the cross wall was a late enlargement, but the outer stair was part of the older work.

From the point at which there may have been, as already said, a doorway in the outer wall, it runs for 53ft in a north-westerly direction as the south wall of a long building of which the major axis is thus inclined and of which the gable-end remains. The east wall projects for 5ft into the court. This long building and the remaining buildings against the outer wall, which proceeds westward for 65ft, seem to have been additions made at earliest in the fourteenth century. Near the north-west and north-east corners of the long building there are traces of other buildings which must have been moved to make room for it. West of this there is an empty space measuring 17ft from east to west and nearly square. To this succeed from east to west three compartments divided by the remaining three party walls. The first, with a cobbled floor, contains an oblong sunken cistern, communicating by a channel which passes through a small archway with a larger cistern at a lower level. The second contains a well, and the third, with a cobbled floor, contains a pear-shaped vat with its narrow end towards the well-chamber. In the west wall of this last compartment, which forms the northward return of the outer wall of the court, there is a wide blocked opening. The wall between the compartment and the court is of one build with the west wall and had a doorway near its east end. It was, however, continued eastward for a short distance between the court and the well-chamber; but of this and of slighter traces of other foundations in this part of the outer court nothing certain can be said.

Outside the west wall of the last compartment there are remains of a building the north and south walls of which are in line with those to the east, but the addition of which was responsible for the blocking of the opening from the inner building. Adjoining this to the north and built against the west wall of the precinct there was another building divided into two rooms, with its longer axis east and west. These buildings may be of post-suppression date: that at the south-west corner has its angle thickened by a large mass of masonry.

Northward of its junction with the west compartment of the south range the west wall of the precinct becomes thicker and proceeds in a straight course to the site of the gatehouse in the north-west corner of the outer court. Parts of the jambs of the doorway remain with the staples for the doors, and a line of wall, north-west of the junction of the gatehouse with the precinct wall, marks the position of the barbican. Inside the doorway a chamfered plinth, with the facing broken away, against the wall of the adjoining brewhouse indicates the extent of the gatehall. There are no traces of the south wall of the gatehouse, but the mention of the "yet-howse tower" in the inventories gives a general indication of its appearance.

CONVERSION TABLE

1ft	0.3m	30yd	27.4m
5ft	1.5m	35yd	32.0m
10ft	3.0m	40yd	36.6m
15ft	4.6m	45yd	41.1m
20ft	6.1m	50yd	45.7m
25ft	7.6m	100yd	91.4m
30ft	9.1m	200yd	182.9m
35ft	10.7m	300yd	274.3m
40ft	12.2m	400yd	365.8m
45ft	13.7m	500yd	457.2m
50ft	15.2m	1000yd	914.4m
100ft	30.5m		
		1 acre	0.40ha
1yd	0.9m	5 acre	2.02ha
5yd	4.6m	10 acres	4.05ha
10yd	9.1m		
15yd	13.7m	1 mile	1.60km
20yd	18.3m	5 miles	8.04km
25yd	22.9m	10 miles	16.09km

Printed in Scotland by Her Majesty's Stationery Office at HMSO Press ,Edinburgh
Dd 289919 K122 10/75 (12708)